SUPERSTARS OF BASEBALL

ALEX RODRIGUEZ

THE RISE TO THE TOP!

A-Rod breaks records and is a baseball superstar!

2011

Helps the Yankees win the World Series.

2009

Rodriguez is sent to the New York Yankees.

2003

The Texas Rangers sign Rodriguez for ten years and $250 million, the biggest contract in baseball history to date.

2001

The Seattle Mariners sign Alex when he is just 17.

1993

Alex's family returns to the United States, where he plays baseball in Miami, Florida.

1982

Family moves to the Dominican Republic.

1979

Alex Rodriguez is born on July 25, in New York City.

1975

Mason Crest
370 Reed Road
Broomall, Pennsylvania 19008
www.masoncrest.com

Printed and bound in the United States of America.

First printing
9 8 7 6 5 4 3 2 1

Library of Congress Cataloging-in-Publication Data

Rodríguez Gonzalez, Tania
 Alex Rodriguez / by Tania Rodriguez.
    p. cm.
 Includes index.
 ISBN 978-1-4222-2674-2 (hardcover) -- ISBN 978-1-4222-2670-4 (series hardcover) -- ISBN 978-1-4222-9163-4 (ebook)
 1. Rodriguez, Alex, 1975---Juvenile literature. 2. Baseball players--United States--Biography--Juvenile literature. I. Title.
 GV865.R62R64 2013
 796.357092--dc23
 [B]

                                    2012020928

Produced by Harding House Publishing Services, Inc.
www.hardinghousepages.com

Picture Credits:
Ben Borkowski: p. 27
Keith Allison: p. 15, 24, 28
Luis Silvestre: p. 6, 7, 8, 10
Mangin, Brad: p. 12, 14, 16, 18, 19, 20, 21, 22, 25, 26, 27

ALEX RODRIGUEZ

Chapter 1

THE BEGINNING

Few sports stars are as famous as Alex Rodriguez. All around the world, baseball fans know the name "A-Rod." They know about his awards and records. They know about the millions of dollars he's paid to play. Rodriguez is so famous, people even know who he's dating! Everything about A-Rod gets into the news!

Alex Rodriguez has been playing baseball in the major leagues for more than fifteen years. In that time, he's played in the *All-Star Game* fourteen times. He's been named *Most Valuable Player (MVP)* three times. His team has won a World Series. A-Rod has done just about everything in baseball.

As a Dominican American, A-Rod was born into a rich baseball *heritage*. For more than a hundred years, baseball has been at the center of Dominican life.

Baseball in the Dominican Republic

The United States brought the game of baseball to Cuba in the mid-1860s; from there, Cuban immigrants, fleeing their country's 10 Years' War in 1868–1878, spread the game throughout the Caribbean, including the Dominican Republic. Dominicans loved the sport right away, and began organizing teams and tournaments. By the 1920s, Dominican teams were competing against other Caribbean

countries and teams in North America.

The game was most popular in the southeast part of the island, where generations of sugarcane worker learned the sport during the working season's down time. The sugarcane factory owners encouraged employees to participate in the sport; the owners even supported the teams financially. This area of the country still produces the greatest number of players who go on to play professionally.

Today Dominican players are on all thirty Major League teams. All major league teams have training camps in the Dominican Republic, to scout and train players for *professional* potential. From dirt diamonds in empty lots to the Stadium Quisqueya, baseball is everywhere on the island. And all around the world, everybody knows—Dominicans are amazing baseball players!

Early Life

Alex Rodriguez was born on July 25, 1975 in New York City. His parents—Victor and Lourdes—were from the Dominican Republic, but they moved to the United States before Alex was born. Victor ran a shoe store in New York City, but he had once been a baseball player in the Dominican Republic. Alex had an older brother, Joe, and an older sister, Suzy.

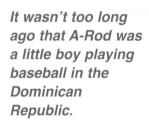

It wasn't too long ago that A-Rod was a little boy playing baseball in the Dominican Republic.

The Dominican Republic may be a poor country, but it has a rich baseball heritage.

In 1979, when Alex was four years old, his family moved back to the Dominican Republic. Alex's father was ready to leave his work at the shoe store in New York City. So he took his family to Santo Domingo. There, Victor ran a pharmacy.

The family lived on the island for three years, but Victor and Lourdes were struggling to earn enough money to support their family. So they decided to move again. When Alex was seven years old, his family moved back to the United States.

Like a lot of boys growing up in the Dominican today, Alex learned to love baseball when he was very young.

Who Are Cal Ripken, Jr. and Keith Hernandez?

Cal Ripken is one of the superstars of the baseball world. He won two MVP awards, set several fielding records, and helped the Baltimore Orioles win a World Series before retiring in 2001. He is famous for his powerful hits.

Keith Hernandez is another baseball superstar. He played for the New York Mets and helped them win the World Series. He played first base and won many awards, including MVP and the Gold Glove.

This time, the family moved to Miami, Florida.

Soon, Victor left the family. Alex had learned a lot from his father, though. Victor had taught him how to play baseball. He had handed down to Alex his love of the game. Alex's heroes were Cal Ripkin, Jr. and Keith Hernandez. He loved the New York Mets.

After her husband left, Lourdes continued to support her son's love of baseball. But she also had to work hard to keep food on the table for the Rodriguez family. As a single mother, Lourdes had to work two jobs to bring in enough money. She worked as a secretary during the day, and at night, she worked as a waitress in a restaurant.

Times were sometimes tough for the family. But they were also important times for young Alex. Later in his life, Alex told *People* magazine about how much he had learned from his mother's hard work. "When Mom got home, I'd always count her tip money to see how good she did," Alex said. "She taught me the meaning of hard work and commitment."

Alex played baseball at the Boys and Girls Clubs of Miami. There, one coach saw that Alex could be a special player. Coach Eddie Rodriguez had the same last name, but he wasn't related to Alex. Soon, though, Eddie was acting like Alex's father. He taught Alex a lot more about baseball. He also helped Alex get through a tough time growing up without his dad around.

As he grew up, baseball was a big part of Alex's life. His best memories were all connected to baseball. It was one of the most important things in his life.

And it always would be!

9

Chapter 2

GOING PROFESSIONAL

As a teenager, Alex went to high school at Westminster Christian High School in Miami. He loved to play on his school's sports teams—and he was really good, too! He played football as well as baseball at Westminster. Alex worked hard to be the best athlete he could be.

In Alex's third and fourth years of high school, the baseball team did very well. Alex played shortstop, and he was one of the team's best players. He won awards and many people started saying that he was destined to be in the Major Leagues when he grew up. Turns out they were right!

Near the end of his time in high school, Alex started looking at colleges. The University of Miami talked to Alex about playing baseball and football for the university, and he liked that idea a lot. He signed a letter saying that he would to the University of Miami.

But, soon, Alex's plans changed. *Major League Baseball (MLB)* scouts had come to watch Alex play. *Scouts* from many different teams had been watching Alex play for Westminster.

In June 1993, Alex was the MLB's top draft pick. The Seattle Mariners drafted Alex when he was just seventeen years old! The offer was just too good to resist—so instead of going to college, Alex would be going to the Major Leagues. His dreams were coming true—and he was still so young!

Alex hadn't heard much from his father in a long time, but the week the Mariners drafted him, his father got in touch with him. Victor had heard on the news about his son being drafted to the Seattle Mariners.

Alex wasn't sure how to feel about his father. He was glad to hear from him after many years, but at the same time, Alex was still hurt that his father had left the family. The man who had given Alex his love for baseball had walked away from him when he was still young. Victor had not been in his son's life much at all for years now—and he still really wasn't there, even as Alex was headed to the Major Leagues. Other people had done more to help Alex get where he was than his father had. Alex felt sad and angry, all at the same time. He went off to the play for the Mariners, feeling proud and happy—but he still had not really made up with his father, and that was a sore spot in his life.

The Minors

When a team drafts a player, he usually starts playing in the team's *minor leagues*. That gives young players more practice. It gives them a chance to improve their skills before they start playing in the big

A-Rod poses with his glove before a game.

leagues. So in 1994, Alex Rodriguez began playing for Seattle's minor-league teams in Wisconsin and Florida. Then he played for the Calgary Cannons. He played so well for the Cannons that he moved up to the Seattle Mariners quickly. By July, Rodriguez was playing in the Major Leagues.

The Majors

When Rodriguez started playing shortstop for the Mariners he was still just eighteen years old! Sadly, Rodriguez's first season didn't last long, because the 1994 baseball players strike ended the season early. Rodriguez only got to play for one month.

And Rodriguez hadn't played as well as his coaches had expected him to. So the Mariners sent him to the Dominican Republic to train. Back on the island, he would play against players from all over the world. He would learn more about playing baseball and get even better. Then he'd come back to Seattle and be the player everyone knew he could be.

Playing in the Dominican Republic wasn't easy for A-Rod.

Alex Rodriguez has become a baseball star.

Many players there were very, very good. Alex told *Sports Illustrated* later in his life that playing in the Dominican Republic was "the toughest experience of my life."

While Alex was in the Dominican Republic, his father showed up at one of his practices. Alex was amazed to look across the field and see his father. He hadn't heard from Victor at all since the week the Mariners drafted him. Alex hadn't

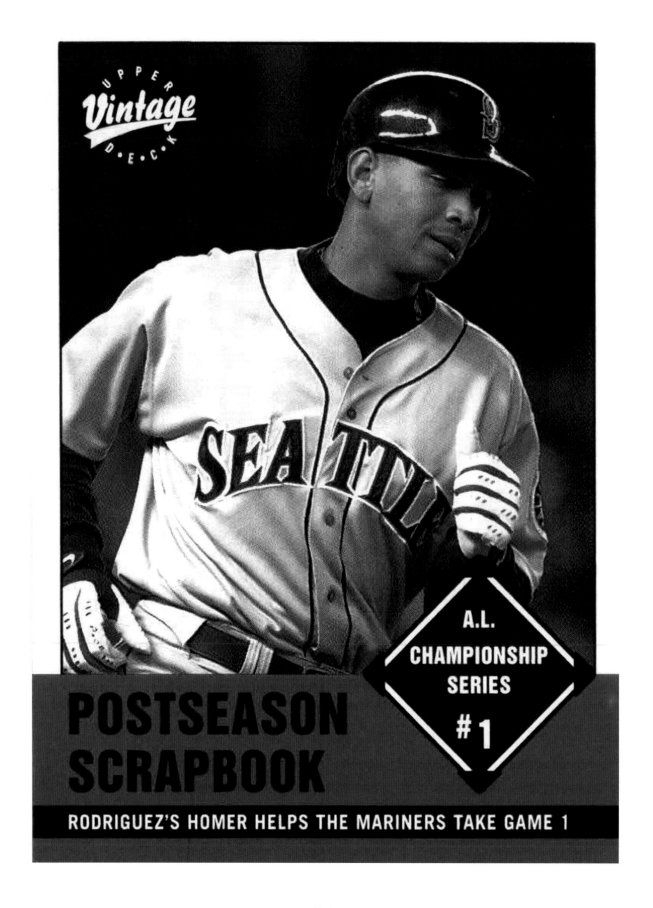

UPPER
Vintage
D•E•C•K

SEATTLE

A.L.
CHAMPIONSHIP
SERIES
#1

POSTSEASON
SCRAPBOOK

RODRIGUEZ'S HOMER HELPS THE MARINERS TAKE GAME 1

even known his father was in the Dominican Republic.

But Alex still didn't know how to feel about the man who had left his family. Victor and Alex talked a little, but they didn't spend much time together. Still, the door in Alex's relationship with his father had opened just a little further. Alex even sent his father a present, once he was back in the States: a satellite dish, so that Victor could watch Mariners games.

By 1995, Alex was back with the Seattle Mariners. But he ended up only spending some of the year playing with the Mariners, and the rest of the season he was with a minor league team in Tacoma, Washington. He went back and forth between the two teams the rest of that year. He played much better than he had the year before, but he still didn't do as well as many people believed he could.

One year later, all that changed. In 1996, Alex played his first full season with the Mariners—and he played as well as anyone could hope, with 36 home runs and 123 *runs batted in (RBIs)*. Fans and baseball writers began to talk about A-Rod being one of the next great players. He played well as shortstop, and he was a great hitter. He knew how to play great baseball, and he was still very young. He was sure to get even better!

Alex came just a few votes short of winning the MLB's 1996 Most Valuable Player (MVP) award. If he had, he would have been the youngest MVP in baseball history. As it was, he was the youngest shortstop to ever play in the All-Star Game. The Associated Press chose Rodriguez as their Major League Player of the Year in 1996.

Alex Rodriguez had become one of baseball's youngest stars. He was on his way now to becoming one of the game's greatest players.

Chapter 3

BECOMING A BASEBALL SUPERSTAR

O ver the next few seasons, Alex played even better. He also became more and more famous. Soon, A-Rod would be one of the most famous players in baseball.

A-Rod talks to the press before a game.

A-Rod in action against the Oakland A's in a 1997 game in California.

Getting Better

In 1998, A-Rod hit 42 home runs. He also stole 46 bases. That meant he was only one of three people in baseball history to get more than 40 home runs and 40 stolen bases in the same year. In 1999, Alex hit 42 home runs again. He'd had to miss many games because of being hurt, too, so the high number of home runs was even more amazing.

In 2000, Alex kept playing well. He hit 41 home runs that year, and the Mariners almost made it to the World Series, too. But the team lost to the New York Yankees in the American League Championship Series.

The 2000 season had been fantastic for A-Rod. He'd played well and he'd almost made it to the World Series. His *contract* with the Mariners ended at the end of the season, and now he was a *free agent* who could be *signed* by any team. And since he was so good, he'd have a lot of choices!

The year 2000 was a good one for Alex for another reason as well. He finally made up with his father. Alex decided he wanted his father in his life again. He was ready to forgive him. He and Victor met on Father's Day, and together they made plans for building a new relationship.

To the Rangers

In 2001, the Texas Rangers signed Alex to a ten-year contract. He would get more than $250 million dollars over ten years. The contract was the biggest in sports history at the time.

Signing to the Rangers didn't change how well Alex Rodriguez played. In fact, he played even better! In 2001, Rodriguez hit 52 home runs. This made him the sixth youngest player to ever hit more

Alex Rodriguez practices before a game.

than 50 home runs in a year. Rodriguez started in every game in the 2001 season. Then in 2002, he did even better. Rodriguez hit 57 home runs and had 142 RBIs. He also won the Gold Glove Award for the first time. This award goes to players who play well on **defense**.

In 2001 and 2002, the Rangers, however, didn't do well in their league. The team finished last both seasons. The team hadn't been winning before Rodriguez came to the team, but A-Rod was supposed to change all that. He was supposed to help the team become great. In 2002, though, it looked like the plan to turn the Rangers around hadn't worked.

In 2003, things didn't look much better. Rodriguez had another great season, but the team still wasn't winning enough games. Alex hit 47 home runs, more than any other player in the American League in 2003. He won the Gold Glove Award again, too, and he also won the Most Valuable Player (MVP) award.

The 2003 season was Alex Rodriguez's last playing for the Rangers. The team decided to **trade** him. At first, the team planned to trade Rodriguez to the Boston Red Sox, but soon, he was traded instead to the New York Yankees. Alex Rodriguez was headed to New York City.

Alex Rodriguez with the Yankees.

A-Rod (right) with his teammate Derek Jeter during a game against the San Francisco Giants.

When Alex joined the Yankees, he had to make some changes. He had to change positions, for one thing. Rodriguez had always played shortstop, but now, he would play third base for the Yankees, since Derek Jeter was already playing shortstop for the team. Alex also had to change the number he wore on his uniform. He'd always before worn number 3, but in New York, number 3 is Babe Ruth's number. No one else can play wearing the number. So, Rodriguez changed his number to 13.

Rodriguez didn't change how well he

Alex Rodriguez's helmet.

Rodriguez plays third base against the Kansas City Royals in a game at Yankee Stadium.

played, though. He kept working hard to be the best player he could be. And now that he was in New York City, he knew there would be millions watching him. He had to make them proud.

Playing with the Yankees

In his first season with the Yankees, Alex Rodriguez played well. He hit 36 home runs and had 106 RBIs. During the season, Rodriguez hit his 350th home run. He was the youngest player to ever hit so many homers. Rodriguez was also chosen for the All-Star game in 2004. He'd been chosen for eight years in a row now!

The Yankees made it to the **playoffs** that year, where they played their long-time rivals the Boston Red Sox. The Yankees ended up losing the American League Championship Series. They wouldn't be going to the World Series.

Alex didn't let the loss affect him, though. Instead, he just worked harder. In

Babe Ruth

George Herman "Babe" Ruth has been called "the most dominant player in history." His record of sixty home runs in one season (1927) was not broken until 1961, when seasons themselves had become longer; and his career record of 714 home runs lasted until 1974, when Hank Aaron hit his 715th home run.

Ruth began as a pitcher for the Boston Red Sox, pitching twenty-nine and two-thirds scoreless World Series innings for them. But the Babe was such a powerful hitter that he was shifted to the outfield, meaning that he could bat in every game. The New York Yankees bought him in 1920 for $125,000 (today worth almost $1.5 million), which proved a wise investment. His four-teen seasons of home runs earned him the title "Sultan of Swat," and Yankee Stadium is still called "the house that Ruth built."

During his career, Ruth scored 2,174 runs and batted in 2,211 more. His slugging average of .847 in 1920 remained the record until Barry Bonds beat it in 2001, with .863. He was so dangerous at the plate that pitchers walked him 2,056 times. Ruth retired in 1935, at the age of 40.

2005, he hit 48 home runs, more than anyone else in the American League. A-Rod also hit his 400th home run during the season. He played so well in 2005 that he was named American League MVP.

In 2006, Rodriguez hit 35 home runs and had 121 RBIs. He was chosen to be an All-Star again, too. He reached 450 home runs during the 2006 season, as well. Though he played well, A-Rod didn't have one of his better seasons in 2006. He knew he could do better. He told reporters that 2006 was one of his toughest seasons in baseball.

In 2007, Rodriguez wanted to turn it all around. And he did!

Chapter 4
A-Rod at the Top

Alex Rodriguez knew he could be a better player—and he made up his mind to prove it! In the first ten games of the season, he hit seven home runs. He hit his 500th home run during the season, too, making him the youngest player to hit 500 home runs. He hit 54 home runs and had more than 150 RBIs. No one else in the league had as many homers or RBIs, and for the third time, Rodriguez won the MVP award.

A-Rod hits a home run!

Special Advisor to the Yankees, Reggie Jackson.

Alex's contract with the Yankees was almost finished, but he didn't want to leave the Yankees. And soon, he and the team had worked out a deal. His new contract would last for 10 years.

In 2008, Rodriguez didn't play as well as he had in 2007. He only hit 35 home runs and had 103 RBIs. Still, Alex Rodriguez was one of the most famous players on the Yankees. He was also one of the most famous players in the entire baseball world. He made the Dominican

Republic proud! His name was known all over the world.

But soon, Alex Rodriguez would be in the news for reasons other than his fame or playing. Trouble was just over the horizon.

Steroids

For many professional players, the pressure to perform well is intense. Athletes face stress from everyone around them to constantly improve their skill, strength, and speed in the game of baseball. From the fans who want their favorite players to win and score good stats, to the coaches and team managers who push their players to perform to their maximum potential, to the players themselves, who are surrounded by other world-class athletes and feel the need to overcome them, the pressure to excel is extreme. Often, an athlete turns to chemical enhancements to reach a level of competitive play that he would not normally be capable of. This is never legal, and is almost always dangerous, but nevertheless, many major-league players feel compelled to participate in performance-enhancing drug use.

The most common performance enhancers are anabolic steroids. These chemicals are similar to testosterone,

A-Rod jokes with his teammates before the 2010 All-Star Game.

which is the male hormone naturally produced by the body to help stimulate muscle growth. That's why when a player takes anabolic steroids, he receives a boost to his speed and strength that is greater than what the body could normally produce on its own. Major League Baseball (MLB), as well as almost every other organized sport, considers this cheating.

Steroids can cause an unhealthy increase in cholesterol levels and an increase in blood pressure. This stresses the heart, and leads to an increased risk of heart disease. Large doses of steroids can also lead to liver failure, and they have a negative effect on blood sugar levels, sometimes causing problems similar to diabetes.

If an adolescent (typically someone under the age of about 17) takes anabolic steroids, the risks are often much worse. Steroids stop bones from growing, which results in stunted growth. In addition, the risks to the liver and heart are much greater, since a young person's liver and heart are not fully matured and are more susceptible to the damage that steroids can cause. Furthermore, taking steroids puts you at a greater risk of psychological problems that generally begin with aggression but often lead to much more serious issues. Considering these health risks, as well as the fact that anabolic steroids are almost universally banned from organized sports, they should not be used, except by those who have legitimate medical conditions that require their use.

In early 2009, *Sports Illustrated* magazine put out a story that said Rodriguez had used steroids in 2003. At first, Rodriguez didn't say anything. But soon, he came out and told the truth. He had used steroids between 2001 and 2003. He stopped using the drugs after spring training in 2003, he said. He blamed himself, saying again and again that he had been "young and stu-

Did You Know?

More injuries happen in baseball and softball than in even the high-contact sports of football, basketball, and hockey. The most common baseball and softball injuries happen to the shoulders and arms because a player makes so many throws. Injuries also occur to the head, knees, and ankles when players collide, runners slide into bases, and fielders dive to make catches. Fractures are common, and many different bones, from fingertips to legs, can be cracked, shattered, or broken.

pid." Unfortunately, not everyone has been able to forgive Alex—and his stupid mistakes will haunt Alex, who's always been concerned about his reputation, for the rest of his life. Many fans wondered whether Rodriguez's career would be hurt by his drug use. But Alex didn't let what others were saying stop him from focusing on baseball. He knew he had made some big mistakes—and now it was time for him to work even harder.

Getting Back on Track

Before the 2009 season started, doctors found a problem with Rodriguez's hip. Rodriguez ended up missing many games with the Yankees because of his hip. When he finally came back, the Yankees were losing too many games. They needed to win more to make it into the playoffs.

Over the course of the season, the Yankees started winning more and more. Rodriguez wasn't playing his best, though. He didn't hit more than 30 home runs in the regular season, and he didn't make it into the All-Star game for the first time in nine years. But the Yankees were doing just fine anyway. By mid-summer, they were in first place in the American League.

The Yankees made it into the playoffs to face the Minnesota Twins. Alex played very well in the playoffs. He helped the Yankees win against the Twins—and now they were heading to the World Series!

The Yankees faced the Philadelphia Phillies in the World Series. The Yankees were ahead for most of the series, and finally, in Game Six, the Yankees beat the Phillies and took the World Series. The Championship win was Alex Rodriguez's first. He'd made it to the top of baseball. He'd broken records and made millions of dollars. And now he'd won his first World Series!

Injuries

In the 2010 season, Rodriguez became the seventh player to hit 600 home runs. He ended the season with 30 home runs and 125 RBIs. Rodriguez hadn't played his very best, but he'd done all right. The 2011 season looked to go well for Rodriguez.

Before the All-Star game, he was playing very well. But around the time he was chosen for the All-Star game, doctors found a problem with his knee. He was put on the *disabled list* and couldn't play in the All-Star game after all.

Rodriguez came back to the Yankees in August, but he hurt his hand in his first game back. After healing up again, Rodriguez was able to finish the season with the Yankees. He hit only 16 home runs and had 62 RBIs. Rodriguez had thir-

The future holds a lot for Alex Rodriguez.

teen years of hitting more than 30 home runs each season. Now, that record had ended.

Alex Rodriguez Today

Ever since he was 18, Alex Rodriguez has worked hard to make his way in Major League Baseball. He's set records and made millions of dollars. He's played for teams across the United States. He's hit more home runs than anyone else his age. There aren't many players as famous as Alex Rodriguez.

No one can say what the future will hold for A-Rod. He's still one of the most successful baseball players ever. He's still a name that millions of people know. Will he win another World Series? Will he win more MVP awards

and break more records? Only time will tell. One thing is for sure, though, A-Rod has become one of baseball's biggest stars.

Inspiring Future Players

The Dominican Republic is proud to claim A-Rod as its own. Alex Rodriguez and all the other Dominican players in the Majors inspire the little boys who play ball in the streets of the Dominican Republic. These boys dream about being the next A-Rod.

But Alex Rodriguez wasn't always the player we know today. He was once just a boy who loved baseball—just like many other little boys growing up in the Dominican Republic today. Who knows which one of them will be the next A-Rod!

Find Out More

Online

Baseball Almanac
www.baseball-almanac.com

History of Baseball
www.19cbaseball.com

Baseball Hall of Fame
baseballhall.org

Major League Baseball
www.mlb.com

Baseball Reference
www.baseball-reference.com

Science of Baseball
www.exploratorium.edu/baseball

Dominican Baseball
mlb.mlb.com/mlb/features/dr/
index.jsp

In Books

Augustin, Bryan. *The Dominican Republic From A to Z.* New York: Scholastic, 2005.

Jacobs, Greg. *The Everything Kids' Baseball Book.* Avon, Mass.: F+W Media, 2012.

Kurlansky, Mark. *The Eastern Stars: How Baseball Changed the Dominican Town of San Pedro de Macorís.* New York: Riverhead Books, 2010.

Glossary

All-Star Game: The game played in July between the best players from each of the two leagues within the MLB.

batting average: A statistic that measures how good a batter is, which is calculated by dividing the number of hits a player gets by how many times he is at bat.

contract: A written promise between a player and the team. It tells how much he will be paid for how long.

culture: The way of life of a group of people, which includes things like values and beliefs, language, food, and art.

defense: Playing to keep the other team from scoring; includes the outfield and infield positions, pitcher, and catcher.

disabled list: A list of players who are injured and can't play for a certain period of time.

division: A group of teams that plays one another to compete for the championship; in the MLB, divisions are based on geographic regions.

free agent: A player who does not currently have a contract with any team.

general manager: The person in charge of a baseball team, who is responsible for guiding the team to do well.

heritage: Something passed down by previous generations.

Major League Baseball (MLB): The highest level of professional baseball in the United States and Canada.

minor leagues: The level of professional baseball right below the Major Leagues.

Most Valuable Player (MVP): The athlete who is named the best player for a certain period of time.

offense: Playing to score runs at bat.

playoffs: A series of games played after the regular season ends, to determine who will win the championship.

professional: The level of baseball in which players get paid.

rookie: A player in his first-year in the MLB.

runs batted in (RBI): The number of points that a player gets for his team by hitting the ball.

scouts: People who find the best young baseball players to sign to teams.

sign: To agree to a contract between a baseball player and a team.

trade: An agreement with another team that gives a player in return for a player from the other team.

Index

Alex Rodriguez